C(
OG
NEWCA

CW00665233

John R. Kenyon BA, ALA, FSA, FRHistS
and C. J. Spurgeon BA, FSA

Contents

*Edited by David M. Robinson BSc, PhD, FSA
and Diane M. Williams BA, MA, PhD
Designed by Staziker Jones
First Published 2001*

© *Cadw: Welsh Historic Monuments (Crown Copyright),
Crown Building, Cathays Park, Cardiff, CF10 3NQ.*

Printed in Great Britain by South Western Printers
ISBN 1 85760 112 2

A late eighteenth-century watercolour of Coity Castle by Paul Sandby (1730/31–1809). Although much of the castle appears as an ivy-clad ruin, the now vanished south gatehouse is shown intact to its full height (Society of Antiquaries of London).

When first established as an earth-and-timber stronghold, probably by William de Londres, Ogmore Castle lay at the westernmost extension of Norman conquest in lowland Glamorgan. Its position, close to the sea and the confluence of the Ogmore and Ewenny rivers, ensured control of these vital routes of communication, as well as supplies for the castle garrison (Crown copyright: Royal Commission on the Ancient and Historical Monuments of Wales).

INTRODUCTION

Although the Norman invaders began to conquer Wales from the later eleventh century, the process by which their Anglo-Norman and English successors aggressively expanded control over the whole of the country took more than two hundred years. In all this time, it was the castle which served as the key to the conquest strategy. At first, strongholds quickly raised in earth and timber provided essential garrison outposts, the centres around which Norman lordships might be established. In later years, great fortresses with curtain walls and towers of stone became the sheet anchors of conquest, and native Welsh leaders found it increasingly difficult to reverse the overwhelming tide of advance.

As a result of this long and often brutal period of conflict, Wales has been left as a land rich in castles. Indeed, in the historic county of Glamorgan alone, up to one hundred sites have been identified. No other part of Wales can match this figure, and few English counties can muster quite as many examples. Although a handful of Glamorgan's castles was built by native Welsh lords in the northern uplands, the majority was first established by Norman conquistadores in the closing years of the eleventh and early twelfth centuries. They were chiefly situated along the coastal belt and in the lower-lying border districts, that is in the most heavily colonized parts of the two great medieval Marcher lordships of Glamorgan and Gower (see map, p. 5).

In terms of their design, Glamorgan's castles vary from humble 'motte-and-bailey' and 'ringwork' structures of the earliest conquest years (many never converted to stone) right through to the magnificence of later thirteenth-century Caerphilly. The three castles which form the subject of this guidebook, however, fall somewhere between these extremes. Coity, Newcastle and Ogmore lie within a few miles of one another in the lower reaches of the Ogmore valley. All three were very probably established at the time of Robert fitz Hamo (d. 1107), the first Norman lord of the formally constituted lordship of Glamorgan. At Coity and Ogmore we can be certain that the initial defences were of earth and timber,

and it seems very likely that the same was true of Newcastle. The defences at all three sites were rebuilt in stone from the early twelfth century onwards.

Seen in the context of the grandest medieval military architecture, none can compare, say, to Chepstow, or perhaps to Edward I's great castles in north Wales. But therein also lies the interest of the group. At Newcastle, for example, we can see a late twelfth-century masonry stronghold totally unencumbered by subsequent building. The same is true of Ogmore, with its masonry largely raised in the twelfth and early thirteenth centuries. Even Coity remained much as rebuilt in masonry in the 1180s for close to two hundred years, and its fourteenth-century refurbishment was concerned far more with domestic accommodation than with military necessity.

There is, then, a strong common link to be found in the sequence of building at all three castles; there is also much that weaves together the strands of their individual histories. In short, although this guide is prepared so that the visitor might discover more of any one of the sites, all three might be explored together as part of a fascinating day's tour.

How this brass mortar came to arrive at Coity is unknown. It is of Islamic form, and was probably used for pharmaceutical purposes. It may have arrived with friends or associates of the Turberville family possibly returning from crusade (National Museum of Wales).

A HISTORY OF THE CASTLES

THE COMING OF THE NORMANS TO THE LATE TWELFTH CENTURY

It is now generally accepted that a castle and mint were established at Cardiff by William I in 1081. William's head appears on this coin of his reign (National Museum of Wales).

Robert fitz Hamo (d. 1107), left, and his son-in-law, Earl Robert of Gloucester (d. 1147), right, were together responsible for the conquest and settlement of much of lowland Glamorgan. They are depicted in stained glass windows at the east end of the abbey church, which fitz Hamo founded at Tewkesbury in 1092 (Vicar and Churchwardens, Tewkesbury Abbey).

It has recently been argued that the initial Norman colonization of Glamorgan was centred on Cardiff. Generally, it is now accepted that it was William the Conqueror (1066–87) who established a castle and a mint on the banks of the Taff in 1081, though there remains some doubt as to just how extensive the early settlement really was and what form it may have taken. Thereafter, in 1093, as part of the widespread advances made by the invaders following the death of the Welsh prince, Rhys ap Tewdwr, it seems that King William II (1087–1100) granted lands in what was soon to become the lordship of Glamorgan to his trusted courtier, Robert fitz Hamo, or Fitzhamon (d. 1107).

Robert moved from his early base in Gloucester. He and his followers annexed and settled the fertile lowlands of Glamorgan as far west as the river Ogmore. Castles were established as part and parcel of the whole process, and among those thrown up during this phase of conquest were Coity, Ogmore and Newcastle. Subsequently, fitz Hamo's son-in-law and successor, Earl Robert of Gloucester, appropriated the western lowlands in the 1120s, establishing further strongholds at Kenfig and Neath. So it was that before the time of Earl Robert's death in 1147, the Norman grip on lowland Glamorgan (*Bro Morgannwg*) was fairly secure. Yet in the uplands to the north (*Blaenau Morgannwg*), native Welsh lords continued to exercise a degree of independent control. In the event, this independence — always nominally subject to the overlordship of the Norman lords of Glamorgan — was retained until the second half of the thirteenth century.

It seems very likely that Robert fitz Hamo established the primary castle at Newcastle by 1106, and in the twelfth century the site was held by the next two lords of Glamorgan, Robert of Gloucester and his son, William, second earl of Gloucester (d. 1183). Meanwhile, the earliest castle at Coity had probably been built at much the same time. It was the only one in this group of three to remain in the hands of a single family throughout most of the Middle Ages, namely the Turbervilles. Finally,

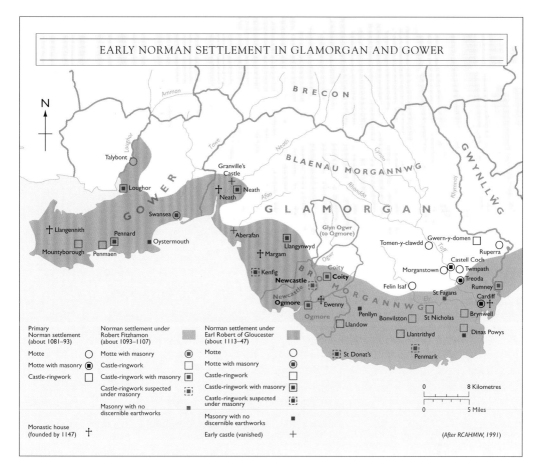

EARLY NORMAN SETTLEMENT IN GLAMORGAN AND GOWER

(After RCAHMW, 1991)

Ogmore Castle — first mentioned when threatened with a Welsh attack in 1116 — appears to have been established by William de Londres, and again it is likely to date from before fitz Hamo's death in 1107.

In terms of their siting, Newcastle stands proud on an escarpment well above the river Ogmore, whereas Coity, which has an elevated view of the Vale of Glamorgan to the south, is overlooked by the ridge of Cefn Hirgoed to the north. Ogmore, in contrast, occupies low ground beside the river Ewenny, just above its junction with the Ogmore. Here, de Londres was able to make full use of water and the adjacent marshland in the defences of his stronghold.

At both Coity and Ogmore, despite the later masonry defences, the layout clearly indicates the form of the original castle. In each case, the earth-and-timber defences were raised in the form of a 'ringwork' — the predominant form of early castle in Glamorgan — and there were no doubt wooden buildings within the ramparts.

Most ringworks tended to be circular enclosures, with the defences surrounding a courtyard or bailey, and sometimes, just as at Coity and Ogmore, there was an additional bailey to one side. This said, it is uncertain whether the fourteenth-century rectangular outer ward at Coity follows the line of an earlier, Norman bailey.

The form of the first castle at Newcastle is less self-evident, but it is generally assumed that the late twelfth-century defences follow the line of a ringwork bank of the conquest era. There may have been a second bailey enclosure surrounding a chapel, later to become the church of St Illtyd which can be seen adjacent to the castle. The only building which survives from this first phase of construction is the hall, situated in the south-east corner of the main bailey. Its rounded corners are comparable to those known at other Norman halls, including the examples at the ringworks of Pennard and Penmaen in Gower.

CASTLES AND THE NORMAN CONQUEST OF LOWLAND GLAMORGAN

King William I (1066–87) himself may have established the motte-and-bailey castle at Cardiff, at the time of his expedition to St Davids in 1081, and it was from here that what became the lordship of Glamorgan was administered. But Cardiff was not alone; immediately to the north and west of the castle there are a number of fortresses, which although undated, may have been established at about the same time (see map p. 5). For how long these earth-and-timber castles remained in use is not known, but it seems likely that some of them were abandoned as the Normans moved further west into Glamorgan.

In the early stages of colonization, the castles were first and foremost fortresses, secure bases from which the chief and lesser lords could defend, exploit and administer their newly acquired territories. Many were built along or close to existing lines of communication, including rivers, coastal routes and former Roman roads, ensuring easy access and safe supply routes. Some, such as at Kenfig, later developed boroughs. Coity, Ogmore and Newcastle, however, never became large centres of settlement, remaining instead as manors and centres of administration once their role as frontier posts had diminished following the westwards expansion of Norman conquest and settlement.

Many of the first castles were mottes or mounds, and there are large numbers of this type of castle in south Wales. But the majority of Norman castles in lowland Glamorgan were

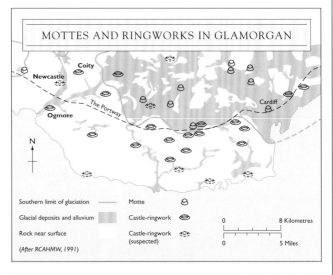

MOTTES AND RINGWORKS IN GLAMORGAN

Southern limit of glaciation	Motte
Glacial deposits and alluvium	Castle-ringwork
Rock near surface	Castle-ringwork (suspected)

(After RCAHMW, 1991)

0 — 8 Kilometres
0 — 5 Miles

The impressive motte, which may have been established by William the Conqueror (1066–87) in 1081, continues to dominate the stronghold at Cardiff. It was from here that the later Norman lordship of Glamorgan was administered.

ringworks — simple earth-and-timber embanked enclosures without the large mound or motte. The reason for this appears to be the geology of the region. Glaciation, with its deep drift deposits, stopped short of the southernmost areas of Glamorgan, especially the Vale. The terrain here consists of a thin covering of soil over limestone, which was not sufficient to erect a large earthen motte. To the north, however, where glacial deposits are abundant, mottes outnumber ringworks.

Following the initial conquest period, the earliest substantial stone building to go up at any of the three sites was at Ogmore, where a small rectangular keep — or main tower — was built on the line of the palisaded ringwork. Up to twelve similar small keeps are known from Glamorgan, in varying states of ruin, with Ogmore as the best preserved example. It may have been built by William de Londres himself, who died about 1126, though a more likely candidate is his son, Maurice (d. 1149), whose handsome tomb can be seen in the church, which his father established at nearby Ewenny.

The keep was raised in very fine dressed stonework or ashlar, quarried not far from Ogmore, at Southerndown. Sutton stone, as it is known, is limestone, which in its freshest state is almost white in colour. Highly prized throughout the Middle Ages, it was used to some degree in all three of the castles considered here. It can be seen, too, at many other Glamorgan strongholds, as well as in churches and monastic houses.

Top: *The priory cell at Ewenny, close to Ogmore Castle, was founded by William de Londres some time before his death in about 1126 and given to St Peter's Abbey in Gloucester. However, it is his son Maurice who is remembered as the founder of the full conventual priory, in 1141. Today, the church remains remarkably unaltered and is an impressive example of Norman ecclesiastical architecture, as shown by this view of the south transept.*

Below: *Maurice's tombstone, carved in the early thirteenth century, lies in the south transept of the priory church at Ewenny and unequivocally records him as 'the founder'.*

A reconstruction drawing of how the Norman keep at Ogmore may have looked when built in the early twelfth century. Entered at first-floor level, what appears as a large, well-appointed chamber was probably divided into two rooms by a timber partition (Illustration by Chris Jones-Jenkins, 2000).

Initially, the Ogmore keep consisted of a first-floor hall, reached by an external staircase, set over a basement. It presumably flanked an original timber gate, though this was replaced in stone in the thirteenth century. At Coity, a similar stone keep was built in the late twelfth century, and this was again positioned beside the gateway. Unlike Ogmore, where a timber palisade was retained alongside the keep for some decades, at Coity the initial stonework was raised in one main phase. Thus, its square keep was structurally integrated from the outset with the polygonal, or faceted, stone curtain wall which replaced the earlier palisade. This work, probably undertaken in the 1180s by Payn de Turberville II (d. 1207), was doubtless a response to the Welsh uprising of 1183–84 that followed the death of Earl William of Gloucester.

The positioning of Norman keeps in an 'offensive' position, that is on the line of the curtain wall or palisade, is common in south Wales, with a notable example to be seen at Usk in Monmouthshire. At Kenfig, on the other hand, the Norman keep was built in the centre of the enclosure. Indeed, the same appears to be true of Newcastle, where there is a record of an early keep, though it had vanished before it was mentioned by the Victorian scholar, G. T. Clark (1809–98), in the 1830s.

The late twelfth century also witnessed the building of the 'cellar' at Ogmore, a free-standing structure in the inner ward opposite the keep, of which only the basement survives. But the most impressive late Norman work in Glamorgan was undoubtedly the extensive rebuilding of Newcastle. The ferocity of the Welsh revolt of 1183–84, following Earl William's death, impelled King Henry II (1154–89) to retain Glamorgan as his own until his death some five years afterwards. Although the accounts of the king's exchequer (the Pipe Rolls) do not mention the work — as they do that at other Glamorgan castles during the 1180s — it seems very likely that the masonry work at Newcastle dates from this short period of royal custody. In fact, we know that the custody of the site at this time was entrusted to Walter Luvel, who received sums for the payment of 300 infantry, and also 60*s*. for the loss of two war-horses.

Just weeks after King Henry II's death in 1189, his younger son, John (d. 1216), married the heiress to the earldom, Isabella of Gloucester (d. 1217), to whom he had been betrothed since 1176. Through his wife, John thus became lord of Glamorgan. And, in an exceptional gesture of conciliation, he ceded Newcastle to Morgan ap Caradog, the leader of the 1183–84 uprising. The castle remained in Welsh hands until 1214, but it seems very unlikely that its advanced masonry defences could have been built during the tenure of the Welsh lords of Afan.

In short, apart from King Henry II, the only other likely builder of the stone defences at Newcastle is Earl William of Gloucester. In this context, we may note that on stylistic grounds the carved masonry of the gateway has been dated to about 1150–80, whereas the castle plan as a whole resembles that at Sherborne Old Castle, in Dorset, also held by Earl William. Sherborne has similar mural towers with battered ashlar plinths, and these were built before 1135 by Roger, bishop of Salisbury (d. 1139). Nevertheless, the form of the Newcastle mural towers can also be paralleled — albeit on a grander scale — by important works undertaken by Henry II at Orford in Suffolk in 1165–73, and at Dover in Kent from 1185.

King Henry II (1154–89) was impelled to hold Glamorgan himself for a period of five years following the Welsh revolt of 1183–84, during which time he may have instigated the building of the stone defences at Newcastle (National Library of Ireland, Ms. 700).

THE THIRTEENTH CENTURY

So, by the turn of the thirteenth century, two of the three castles (Coity and Newcastle) had been comprehensively refurbished in masonry, each with a small keep and walled perimeter, and Newcastle had the added sophistication of two square mural towers. The third castle, Ogmore, also had its stone keep and an internal masonry structure, but its remaining defences were still of earth and timber.

From 1217, Newcastle was held by the Turbervilles and it was to survive largely unchanged during the ensuing centuries. This said, a hall was added to the north of the earlier round-cornered domestic structure in the thirteenth century. In addition, the remains of a building on the north side of the courtyard may belong to the later Middle Ages, although it could equally have been part of the refurbishment

Architectural parallels for Newcastle have been identified at both Sherborne Old Castle (top), built by Bishop Roger of Salisbury (d. 1139) and later held by Earl William of Gloucester (d. 1183), and at Dover, Kent (above), where Henry II undertook important works after 1185 (© Skyscan Balloon Photography. Source: English Heritage).

undertaken here in the sixteenth century (see p. 16). Moreover, it was not until the next century that the Turbervilles and their successors undertook much in the way of building improvements to their main seat at Coity.

Only at Ogmore were significant works undertaken in the thirteenth century. To begin with, its palisaded ring-bank was replaced by a masonry curtain wall, but without mural towers. So as to provide a level platform for the stone curtain, the ring-bank was partly levelled, and the resulting spoil was spread across the inner ward, levelling up the interior. A simple masonry gate-tower was provided beside the keep, with a bridge pit in front of it, and wing or spur walls ran from the new curtain across the ditch to the outer ward opposite. The domestic arrangements of the keep were enhanced by the addition of an upper storey and a latrine turret built against the north-west corner. A newel stair was inserted in this corner too, linking the upper floors of the keep, and providing access to the new latrines.

Domestic improvements during this period at Ogmore were not limited to the new works on the keep. Indeed, a rectangular hall was constructed on the north side of the inner bailey, utilizing the curtain wall for its north and east walls; only the lowest courses of masonry survive. Although evidence for the kitchen block is slender, footings of a building immediately to the north of the keep lie under the grass, conveniently placed to serve as a kitchen for both keep and hall. On the opposite side of the ward to the hall lay a smaller, subdivided, rectangular building, the function of which is uncertain.

The defences of the outer ward at Ogmore were never rebuilt in stone, but excavations in 1949 revealed a sequence of internal stone buildings. The earliest of these buildings was denoted by the vestiges of a rectangular thirteenth-century structure. This had fallen out of use around the end of that century when a small limekiln was built over it, presumably for the production of building mortar. Interestingly, similar kilns may be seen at

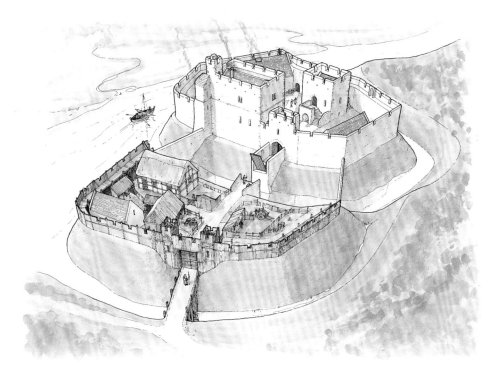

Ogmore Castle was substantially remodelled in the early thirteenth century, when the ring-bank of the inner ward was flattened to make way for a new stone curtain and gate-tower. The keep was also modified and a new stone hall built in the north-east corner of the ward. The defences of the outer ward were never rebuilt in stone, but, as suggested in this reconstruction of how the castle may have looked at this time, there is some evidence for internal stone buildings (Illustration by Chris Jones-Jenkins, 2000).

other castles in Wales, including Carreg Cennen in Carmarthenshire and Cilgerran in Pembrokeshire. At Ogmore, it was at about this time, too, that a small stone gateway was inserted in the north rampart of the outer ward.

In considering who was responsible for these thirteenth-century improvements at Ogmore, we may note that on the death of Thomas de Londres — great-grandson of the first Norman lord of Ogmore — the castle passed in about 1216 to his daughter Hawise (d. 1274). She had three husbands: Walter de Braose, who was possibly killed in the Welsh war of 1233–34; Henry de Turberville of Coity, who died before 1240; and Patrick de Chaworth, who was killed fighting the Welsh in 1258. The simple nature of the masonry defences denote work of the early thirteenth century, presumably by Thomas de Londres or in the time of Hawise and Walter de Braose.

Hawise's sons by her third marriage, Payn (d. 1279) and Patrick de Chaworth (d. 1283), were successively lords of Ogmore, and were also responsible for the construction of the impressive inner ward at Kidwelly Castle in Carmarthenshire. In the event, some eight years after Patrick's death, in 1291, his daughter Matilda (or Maud) was granted in marriage by King Edward I to Henry (d. 1345), the second son of Edmund, earl of Lancaster (1267–96). The ceremony, however, did not take place until 1298. Nonetheless, this marriage began the chain of events which took the lordship of Ogmore into the duchy of Lancaster, and so eventually into the hands of the Crown, when Henry of Lancaster became King Henry IV in 1399.

Payn (d. 1279) and Patrick de Chaworth (d. 1283), the sons of the de Londres heiress, Hawise (d. 1274), each held Ogmore, but appear to have lavished their attention on Kidwelly Castle where they built the impressive inner ward. The seal of Patrick appears on this manuscript dated 1281 (Public Record Office, DL 27/57).

When the daughter of Patrick de Chaworth married Henry (d. 1345), the second son of the earl of Lancaster, so began a chain of events which took the lordship of Ogmore first into the duchy of Lancaster, and then into Crown hands, when Henry of Lancaster became King Henry IV in 1399 (British Library, Harleian Ms. 4380, f. 186v).

THE FOURTEENTH CENTURY

During the fourteenth century, the Turberville family made a number of major improvements to the stronghold at Coity, though sadly it is not possible to date the various phases of rebuilding very closely. It appears that the castle had remained unchanged since the late twelfth century, unless the large rectangular foundation in the inner ward dates to the intervening period.

Now, in the fourteenth century, the outer ward was enclosed with a masonry wall, itself incorporating a series of square or rectangular towers. On the north side, this curtain wall ran across the inner ditch to meet the existing masonry of the inner ward. In contrast, the cross-wall on the south side appears to be a work of the fifteenth century. Either it replaced a timber palisade which for some reason persisted throughout the fourteenth century, or perhaps the later cross-wall was built to take the place of one which may have been seriously damaged in the sieges of 1404–05 (p. 14). Another major feature of the fourteenth-century work was the building of the middle gate.

THE LORDSHIP OF OGMORE

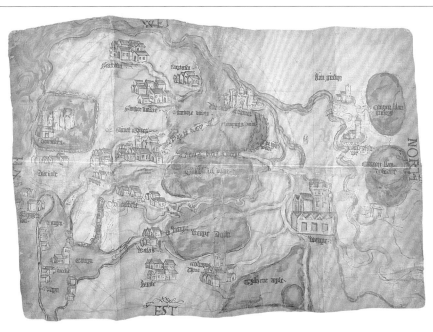

A sixteenth-century map of the lordships of Ogmore, Dunraven and Ewenny. Ogmore Castle can be seen in the centre towards the top of the map, alongside the river Ewenny (Public Record Office, MR 6, from DL 31/58).

The lordship of Ogmore was one of the more prosperous of the constituent lordships of Glamorgan. It was, however, divided into two parts; part located in the upland or *Blaenau Morgannwg*, which remained strongly Welsh in character, and part in the lowland — *Bro Morgannwg*. It was here, on the more fertile land of the Vale, that Anglo-Norman settlement was concentrated and a system of English tenure was introduced.

The ownership of land in *Bro Morgannwg* was vested in the lord of Ogmore, his immediate followers, (what later became the gentry), as well as in the Church, especially nearby Ewenny Priory. Work on the land itself was undertaken by tenants, both free and unfree, and although it is likely that the majority of those who farmed the land initially were Welsh, it was perhaps with good reason that the *Bro* gradually

became known as the Englishry.

In return for their position, the lords of Ogmore owed feudal duties to their overlord, which included the service of four knights to Cardiff Castle. Likewise the tenants of the lords of Ogmore often held their lands in return for such duties — a pattern that persisted well into the thirteenth century, primarily because of the threat of Welsh attack. It was clearly a society organized for defence if not for war.

The fourteenth century witnessed profound changes to the lordship, when in 1345 it finally became part of what was to become the duchy of Lancaster, which controlled lands from Monmouth to Kidwelly in Wales, as well as large estates in England. In addition, there were a number of bad harvests, the Black Death of 1349 that led to the depopulation of many areas, and the Glyn Dŵr uprising, which

caused much damage to property.

Recovery was slow, though a smaller population meant that more land was available at cheaper rents and a number of men took full advantage of this to become wealthy farmers. It was these far-sighted individuals, together with those old established families that remained in the area, which formed the nucleus of the emerging Glamorgan gentry. With the new lords of Ogmore resident in England, it was left to the men on the ground to administer the estates, and it was these gentry families that were to play an increasing role in local and national affairs in the fifteenth and sixteenth centuries.

This was to serve as the new entrance from the outer to the inner ward, providing a stronger defensive feature as well as improving the approach to the heart of the castle.

Much of the rest of the fourteenth-century building programme was aimed at enhancing the domestic accommodation at the site. The Norman keep, for example, was altered considerably; its interior was rebuilt with vaulted floors, and an annexe was added on its north side to provide a latrine block, all of which implies that the structure continued to serve as private accommodation for the lords of Coity. At the same time, a new range of domestic apartments was raised on the southern side of the inner ward, including a first-floor hall set over a vaulted basement, together with a kitchen. A projecting tower was built out from the curtain, though not for defence purposes but to house a suite of latrines.

Interestingly, one feature of this domestic building programme at Coity proved abortive. The overall plan envisaged a chapel, which was to extend beyond the curtain wall through a proposed breach in the earlier Norman masonry. The planning of this scheme is indicated by a corbel, with ribs, set into the wall of the grand staircase as part of what was to have been a vaulted chamber beneath the chapel, and by the fine vaulted stair leading down to that aborted undercroft. But the work for some reason was not carried through to completion.

Such is the scale of this rebuilding at Coity that it seems likely that more than one Turberville lord oversaw the various works. The scheme may have been initiated by Payn de Turberville III (about 1283–1318), who served as seneschal of Cardigan, and briefly as the royal keeper of Glamorgan following the death of Gilbert de Clare, earl of Gloucester, in 1314. Indeed, as custodian of the lordship, it was Payn's unsympathetic handling of the native Welsh in upland Glamorgan which did much to incite the furious rebellion led by Llywelyn Bren in 1316. But most of the fourteenth-century reconstruction at Coity was probably undertaken during the long tenure of Payn's son, Gilbert IV, who held the castle from about 1318 to about 1349. Certainly, by the 1380s, when the castle had passed to Sir Lawrence Berkerolles (d. 1411), son of one of the Turberville co-heiresses, it constituted a splendid fortified mansion, fit even for King Richard II (1377–99) who stayed there in September 1394 *en route* for Ireland.

The tomb effigy of Payn de Turberville III (about 1283–1318) in the church of St Mary, alongside Coity Castle. He may have been responsible for part of the major fourteenth-century building work at the castle, which included the construction of the southern domestic range and the addition of an annexe to the keep (Vicar and Churchwardens, St Mary's Church, Coity).

The tomb effigies of Katherine de Turberville of Coity and Sir Roger Berkerolles of East Orchard (d. 1351) in St Athans church, Vale of Glamorgan. When the last Turberville lord of Coity died without an heir, the inheritance passed to Katherine's son, Sir Lawrence Berkerolles, who held the castle until his death in 1411 (Vicar and Churchwardens, St Tathan's Church, St Athan).

As for Ogmore, although it is difficult to ascribe very much of the later medieval construction work to a particular century, documentary evidence does shed some light on building during this period. In 1380–81, for example, the duchy of Lancaster accounts show that a carpenter spent fifty-three days erecting a timber butchery and pantry to serve the hall, the timber coming from the Neath area. This record reminds us that the ruins of any castle are but the bare skeleton of its former glory, with timberwork and more ephemeral buildings having long since disappeared.

THE FIFTEENTH CENTURY

Both Ogmore and Coity suffered serious damage during the Owain Glyn Dŵr uprising of the early fifteenth century, notably in the years 1402–05. Indeed, a 1428 survey of the lordship of Ogmore goes as far as to state:

Top: *The building identified as the Court House in the outer ward of Ogmore Castle would have been used for the administration of justice in the lordship.*

Below: *A prisoner in shackles kneels before a judge (British Library, Harley Ms. 4375, f.140).*

'the castle of Ogmore is not worth as much as it costs in repair because it was destroyed in the time of the rebellion'. Nevertheless, consequent repairs to the castle seem to have been undertaken fitfully over the decades following the rebellion, judging by the duchy of Lancaster records which cover the lordship. A building referred to as the 'knighting chamber' was burnt, although it was not repaired until 1442–44. The chamber was possibly part of the hall, in which case the repairs could be represented by the south wall, much of which is a late medieval rebuild. The bridge fronting the castle gate had already been patched up in 1429–30, and ridge-tiles had been purchased to repair the roof of the chapel (location unknown) and other unspecified towers in 1441–42. Refurbishment of the castle continued into the 1450s, with a total expenditure of £31 10s. 1d.

But the most significant late medieval building at Ogmore is situated in the outer ward, namely the Court House. The present structure seems to be that which was repaired at a cost of £2 7s. 2d. in 1454–55, though its origins could go back to the previous century. In fact, given its orientation and window details, it is just feasible that the building was first raised as a chapel. Nevertheless, later documentary evidence makes it clear that between 1454 and 1803 it was being used for court sessions. When, in 1803, J. T. Barber published his account of his tour through south Wales, he described the Court House as a 'thatched hovel ... which appears like an overgrown pig-stye', where manor courts were still held. Other late medieval work includes the two rooms on either side of the steps leading down into the 'cellar' in the inner ward, opposite the keep.

Although there is no record of the capture of Coity during the Glyn Dŵr uprising, the protracted assaults of 1404 and 1405 left the castle extensively damaged. In 1404, a Commons plea was made to the king for a relief force to be sent to assist Sir Lawrence Berkerolles. Royal instructions were issued, and a force was duly assembled at Hereford in November of that year under the king's sons. The sheriff of Warwickshire was instructed to provide twenty men-at-arms and two hundred archers from the county, all well equipped. Similar instructions raised forces in the counties of Worcester, Gloucester, Stafford and Wiltshire, with the whole campaign costing just over £783.

OWAIN GLYN DŴR

An account by Edward Williams, perhaps better known as Iolo Morganwg (1747–1826), records that Owain Glyn Dŵr visited Coity in disguise, and that he was lavishly entertained by Sir Lawrence Berkerolles, its lord, for some days. Upon his departure, Owain revealed his true identity, whereupon Sir Lawrence was struck dumb, never to speak again. Whether or not there is any truth in the story is not known, but the tale demonstrates the enduring quality of the myths that surround the memory of Owain Glyn Dŵr. The man himself, however, remains something of a shadowy and elusive figure.

Owain was born about 1359 and could claim princely ancestry through both his parents. Educated at the Inns of Court, London, he progressed from legal student to squire and soldier, serving in the Scottish campaigns and elsewhere. But by 1400 he was comfortably established as a respected Welsh country gentleman with residences at both Sycharth and Glyndyfrdwy. Wales, however, was less settled at this time. Rising discontent — initially a result of local land disputes induced in part by the overthrow of Richard II (1377–99) — led members of the gentry to contemplate rebellion and in September 1400 Owain was proclaimed prince of Wales.

The Welsh, particularly skilled in the art of guerrilla warfare, achieved some notable successes in the early years of the revolt. They won the battle of Bryn Glas, near Pilleth, Powys in 1402, inflicted considerable damage on many towns, including Kidwelly

Coity Castle was twice besieged by Owain Glyn Dŵr, in 1404 and 1405. This fifteenth-century manuscript illustration shows the siege of Mortagne in 1378 in which Owain Lawgoch, the last descendant of the princely line of Gwynedd, died. His death later enabled Owain Glyn Dŵr to proclaim himself as his legitimate heir to the title prince of Wales (British Library, Royal Ms 14E. IV, f. 23).

and Cardiff, and took some of the strongest castles in Wales, most famously Aberystwyth and Harlech. Indeed, royal forces had to relieve Coity twice, such was the military strength at Owain's disposal. However, even with French and Breton military support, the tide began to turn around 1405, following an English victory near Usk. With the recapture of Aberystwyth and Harlech by the Crown between 1408 and 1409, the revolt was almost at an end. Owain himself rapidly faded from the annals and by 1416 was probably dead.

A replica of the great seal of Owain Glyn Dŵr as independent prince of Wales, about 1405 (National Museum of Wales).

Almost a year later, in September 1405, a further relief force was required. It was led by King Henry IV himself, but it proved a total failure largely due to bad weather.

If the precise fate of the Coity garrison is uncertain, structural evidence clearly indicates severe damage to the castle fabric as a result of the ferocity of the Welsh attacks. Most damage was inflicted on the vulnerable north side, facing the high ground where the Welsh concentrated their efforts. Earthworks which were once prominent in this area — presumed to be siegeworks — are now largely levelled. Certainly the northern section of the faceted Norman curtain wall of the inner ward had to be replaced by a length of straight wall, with a new gate-tower at its eastern end. Yet this gate, with its well-lit chambers, was built more as a feature of prestige than one of serious defence purpose. Further repairs were needed in the outer ward, where a central section of the north wall had to be rebuilt.

Later in the fifteenth century, the chapel at Coity, which had earlier been abandoned, was finally completed. Set over a vaulted basement, it was to abut the grand stair of the hall-block. Before the close of the century its roof-line and east window had been raised, and a stair block was built against the north corner.

The other significant fifteenth-century developments at Coity took place in the outer ward, where a large barn with a porch was erected against the south curtain wall. Both the outer curtain and the internal wall of the barn were buttressed to sustain the substantial timbers of a roof spanning the broad interior. The barn appears to have been intact in the early nineteenth century. Elsewhere in the outer ward, the south tower was converted into a gatehouse, and from this gate a new stone cross-wall was carried across to the inner ward, incorporating a number of loops which seem to have been designed for handguns. This wall was heightened at a later date, encasing its original crenellations. Assuming the ditch of the inner ward was still open, the loopholes must have been reached from a timber platform. Finally, the west gate was rebuilt in a simple form, along with a new south-west tower, seemingly housing a watermill, and replacing the adjacent tower which now made way for a postern.

Some of the above repairs were undertaken by Sir Lawrence Berkerolles, but most of the new buildings are best attributed to the Gamage family. The Gamages succeeded Sir Lawrence through marriage with the Turberville family. In the fourteenth century, a William Gamage had married Sarah, the fourth daughter of Payn de Turberville III. Their grandson, Sir William Gamage (d. 1419), became the first of that family to hold Coity.

THE SIXTEENTH CENTURY AND LATER

The Gamages made modest internal improvements at both Coity and Newcastle in the sixteenth century. At Newcastle, these works are now represented by the transomed Elizabethan windows with square heads, and by a ground-floor fireplace, all inserted into the south tower by John Gamage (d. 1584). The details confirm the evidence of a manuscript compiled in 1596–1600 by Rice Lewis, which describes the castle as 'a pretie pile newly begun to be reedified by John Gamadge esquiour'.

The accommodation in the inner ward at Coity was also improved; new windows and fireplaces were installed on the upper floors of the south range. In the kitchens, a transverse cross wall was introduced, incorporating

The Gamage family succeeded Sir Lawrence Berkerolles and retained the lordship of Coity until about 1584. This plaque, showing the Gamage coat-of-arms, is reset in the wall of a house facing the south side of the castle (Crown copyright: RCAHMW).

A reconstruction of Coity Castle as it may have looked following the sixteenth-century refurbishment. The ditch between the outer ward (foreground) and the inner ward (background), here shown open, was probably filled in sometime during this century (Crown copyright: RCAHMW).

Above: Coity and Newcastle passed to the Sidney family on the marriage of Barbara Gamage (d. 1621) to Robert Sidney, later earl of Leicester (1618–26), as he is seen here. The Sidneys maintained Coity sufficiently well to accommodate a younger son, Jocelyn Sidney, in the early years of the eighteenth century; however, by 1833, when the castle passed to the earl of Dunraven, it was described as 'extensive and magnificent even in its ruins' (National Portrait Gallery, London).

Below: The south front of Coity Castle by Samuel and Nathaniel Buck, 1740. Despite the depredations of stone robbers, the castle appears remarkably complete.

fireplaces and ovens, and a new stair was to lead up from this area. The upper floors of the keep were also refenestrated, and together with its north annexe it was raised a further storey. In particular, it is the arch-headed, hollow-chamfered Tudor windows which attest to the date of this Coity refurbishment, the work perhaps being undertaken by John Gamage's grandfather, Sir Thomas. In passing, we might also note that it was possibly in the sixteenth century that the section of ditch between the two wards at this castle was filled in.

It may well have been the early sixteenth-century refurbishment at Coity which was noticed by the antiquary John Leland in the 1530s, when he stated that 'This castelle is maintainid ...'. Leland did not record any observations at Newcastle, but he said of Ogmore that it was 'meatly welle maintainid'. Later, however, when the lordship of Ogmore was surveyed in 1631, the castle had apparently been in a state of decay for some years. The only building in regular use was the Court House in the outer ward. Newcastle was probably abandoned around much the same time. In 1584, the much sought after Gamage heiress, Barbara (d. 1621), married Robert Sidney, later the earl of Leicester (1618–26). Robert's father, Sir Henry, was the lord president of the Council in the Marches of Wales, based at Ludlow Castle; his elder brother, Philip, was the famous Elizabethan courtier. The Sidneys seems to have

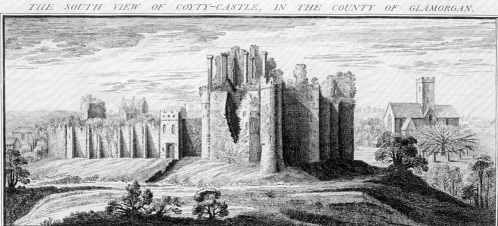

THE SOUTH VIEW OF COYTY-CASTLE, IN THE COUNTY OF GLAMORGAN.

THIS Castle is Situated about 2 Miles from the Rivers Ogmore and Evenny, about 3 Miles northward of Bridgend. It was given by Robert Fitz-Hamond to Sʳ Paine Turbervile, at the Conquest of Iestin ap Gurgan Lord of Glamorgan, &c A.D.1091. and is now the Possession of Charles Edwin, Esqʳ

Samˡ & Nathˡ Buck delin.et Sculp. Publish'd according to Act of Parliament. April 5ᵗʰ 1740.

This eighteenth-century watercolour of Ogmore Castle by Paul Sandby (1730/31–1809) is painted in the 'Picturesque' tradition and depicts the castle in a ruinous condition (Society of Antiquaries of London).

maintained Coity until the middle of the eighteenth century, but neglected Newcastle.

None of the three castles seems to have played any part in the Civil War between king and parliament in the 1640s, and gradually they fell into decay, their stone being used for other purposes. In the time between a visit to Coity by G. T. Clark in 1832, and the published account (1877) of the scholar's investigations at the site, significant sections of masonry had fallen. In the meantime, the interior of Newcastle was serving as a garden, becoming a market garden shortly before the First World War. At Ogmore a nineteenth-century limekiln was built in the 'cellar' building.

These years of neglect came to an end when the three sites were taken into the care of the State: Ogmore in 1928, Coity in 1929, and Newcastle in 1932. They have since been conserved and maintained and are now in the care of Cadw: Welsh Historic Monuments.

Ogmore Castle, prior to conservation work, which began after the site was taken into State care in 1928.

19

A BIRD'S-EYE VIEW OF COITY CASTLE
FROM THE NORTH

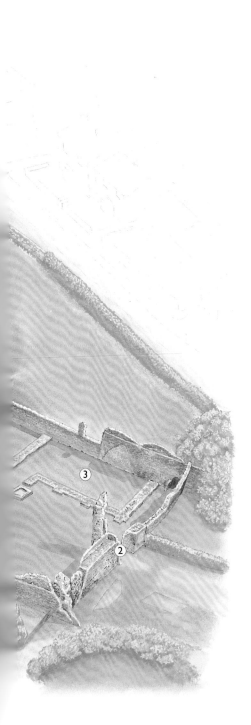

1 **Outer ward** — *surrounded by a curtain wall of varying thickness, and towers dating principally from the fourteenth century, the outer ward would probably have contained a number of service buildings (pp. 11, 22–4).*

2 **West gatehouse** — *vestiges of the simply defended fifteenth-century gatehouse, probably built following the Glyn Dŵr sieges (pp. 16, 22).*

3 **Barn** — *the foundations of a massive fifteenth-century barn, which once dominated the outer ward (pp. 16, 24).*

4 **South gatehouse** — *built first as a tower in the fourteenth century, the south gatehouse was remodelled as such in the fifteenth century. Eighteenth-century illustrations show it virtually intact (pp. 16, 18, 25).*

5 **North tower** — *badly damaged during the Glyn Dŵr sieges, little survives of the original fourteenth-century tower (p. 25).*

6 **Inner ward** — *the heart of the castle protected by the faceted Norman curtain wall and originally surrounded by a ditch. The foundations of a large rectangular building of unknown purpose dominate the courtyard (pp. 26, 29).*

7 **Middle Gatehouse** — *built on the site of the original Norman gateway, the fourteenth-century gatehouse was approached via a drawbridge across a ditch (now filled in) and defended by a portcullis and heavy double doors (pp. 11–12, 26–7).*

8 **Keep** — *the Norman keep was substantially remodelled in the fourteenth century when two elaborate stone-vaulted ceilings were inserted and an annexe was built. Another floor was added to both buildings in the sixteenth century (pp. 8, 13, 18, 27–9).*

9 **North-east gatehouse** — *Coity's most impressive feature, the fifteenth-century gatehouse with its fine 'machicolated' parapet, was probably built as much to impress as defend (pp. 16, 30–1).*

10 **Chapel** — *the chapel block was originally planned to project beyond the line of the curtain wall, but was completed to a more modest scheme in the fifteenth century (pp. 13, 16, 31–2).*

11 **Hall block** — *the hall was situated above a vaulted undercroft at the heart of the fourteenth-century south range and approached via an impressive vaulted lobby and grand stair (pp. 13, 34–5).*

12 **Latrine tower** — *this impressive tower was built principally not for defence but to provide latrines for the adjacent chambers in the south range (pp. 13, 35–6).*

13 **Service range** — *kitchen facilities, including a malting kiln, double oven and fireplace, are located at ground-floor level. Begun in the fourteenth century, both the kitchen area and chambers above were refurbished during the sixteenth-century improvements to the south range (pp. 13, 16–18, 33–4).*

(Illustration by Dale Evans)

A TOUR OF COITY CASTLE

Coity Castle is located on a low ridge with far reaching views over the Vale of Glamorgan. The earliest earth-and-timber stronghold was gradually rebuilt in stone and, by the sixteenth century, the castle could offer sumptuous accommodation as well as security.

THE OUTER WARD

The small car park for the castle at Coity is situated at the western end of the stronghold. The large grass-covered outer ward lies in the foreground, and beyond you will see the more prominent walls of the defences and domestic ranges of the inner ward. Most of the outer ward curtain wall, together with its towers, dates from the fourteenth century. At this point, however, the castle is entered through the vestiges of the fifteenth-century west gatehouse.

The West Gatehouse

The original gateway into the outer ward may have been severely damaged during the two Welsh sieges in 1404–05 (p. 14), necessitating a rebuild. Part of the north wall of the bailey of the ward certainly had to be rebuilt following these sieges. Originally, a ditch fronted the west and north sides of the outer ward, but this has long since been infilled. The ditch to the south can still be seen.

The rebuilt west gatehouse was not a particularly strong building. It was small and ill-designed for defence, even in comparison with the weak but ostentatious contemporary gatehouse on the north-east side of the inner ward. The gate-passage was formerly barrel vaulted but lacked a portcullis, and it was simply closed by centrally placed doors. Sufficient fabric survives in one corner of the first floor to provide an indication of the form of the upper levels. The first floor was lit by a window in its east wall, overlooking the outer ward, and no doubt there was an equivalent window in the west wall to cover the approaches to the gate. This upper room had a timber ceiling supported on projecting stone corbels. Above, a cramped attic floor is indicated by the survival of one side of a small window in the east wall.

The first floor of the gate was approached, from the south, by way of the fourteenth-century flight of steps seen against the inner face of the curtain wall. There was no access from the gate out on to the curtain wall to its north.

The Curtain Wall

You should now enter the outer ward and begin by observing the details of the enclosing curtain wall. It varies in thickness, being stronger on the more vulnerable western and northern sides. The south wall, at less than 3 feet (0.9m) in width, and later incorporated into a barn,

The outer ward of the castle was fortified in stone mainly in the fourteenth century. Subsequent alterations and additions included the construction of a massive barn in the fifteenth century, the foundations of which are visible in the foreground.

The south-west corner of the outer ward, where the fourteenth-century mural tower was replaced by a postern and turret, which projects into the adjacent garden. The footings of the barn are in the foreground.

The Barn

The barn, once a handsome fifteenth-century building, must have dominated the outer ward. It seems to have survived intact into the nineteenth century, when Walter Davies, in his published survey of the agriculture of south Wales (1815), mentions the tradition that 'it was originally the Westminster-Hall of the Coety Lordship'. One side of the barn was formed by the fourteenth-century curtain wall, though the thrust of the roof caused the masonry to lean outwards, necessitating some refacing at the western end where several external buttresses were raised to match those of the newly built inner wall. The entrance porch projects into the centre of the ward and accommodates a small chamber on the right-hand side, perhaps used by an official overseeing storage arrangements. Two doors in the side walls of the porch may have ensured the necessary draught required for the threshing process. The date of the cross-wall within the barn cannot be easily determined.

Notice that the east gable end of the barn abuts a fourteenth-century flight of steps which led up into the south tower and on to the original adjacent parapet. Nearby, the stub of walling which projects out from the gable end cannot be readily dated or explained.

is rather thinner. The builders correctly predicted that any assaults would be launched from the higher ground to the north, as proved to be the case in 1404–05. One should also bear in mind that the south curtain faced falling ground and was well flanked by the south-west and south towers; the north curtain only had one tower, although its wall-walk was overlooked by the keep.

In the far north-west corner of the ward, there is a small doorway or postern. The blocking conceals the sockets for the wooden drawbar once used to keep it fast. A plan of 1877, by G. T. Clark, shows a rectangular building standing in this same general area, running from the outer (west) gate to the northern curtain wall.

On the other side of the outer gatehouse, in the south-west corner, there is a doorway or postern now blocked with a metal grille. A foundation wall behind the postern, together with external stubs of masonry, denote the position of the fourteenth-century south-west tower straddling the curtain. It was dismantled in the fifteenth century, when the postern was introduced, and was replaced by the existing turret which projects into a private garden (p. 37) from the west wall. The turret has narrow windows, and there is a large blocked opening set very low down in its south wall. The opening suggests that — although it is now filled in — water once flowed along the west ditch, passing through the deeply-founded cellar in the turret, possibly as part of a mill complex. Further indication of the management of the ground-water is denoted by the sluice in the bridge over the south ditch (p. 37).

The South Gatehouse

In the fourteenth-century castle, on the south side of the outer ward, a tower straddled the eastern end of the defences. It was contemporary with the tower on the opposite curtain and with that in the south-west corner of the ward. Only the lower courses of the south tower survive, retaining vestiges of a loop in the south-east corner. Its upper floor was reached by an external stair, later incorporated into the barn. There are traces of a recessed latrine which served this upper chamber on the west side of the tower, and its outfall is visible externally where the tower meets the curtain wall.

In the fifteenth century, this tower was converted into a gatehouse. One pier of the inserted gate-passage survives on the west side, incorporating traces of a stair to the upper floor at its southern end. The south gatehouse was still virtually intact in the eighteenth century, as witnessed by the engraving published by the Buck brothers in 1740. It is seen even more clearly in a 1772 watercolour by Paul Sandby (1730/1–1809), engraved in 1774. There was an off-centre doorway in the gatehouse, with two trefoil-headed windows above, the whole surmounted by a corbelled and crenellated parapet, within which a gabled roof with chimney ran east–west.

The wall with distinctive cross-loops, which runs between the south gatehouse and the inner ward, is discussed more fully below (p. 37).

The North Tower

As you cross the outer ward, towards the remains of the north tower on the opposite side, notice the rebuilt central section of curtain wall to your left. The wall and its parapet were repaired following the sieges of 1404–05. A doorway into the north tower, with provision for a drawbar, gave access to the basement. Immediately inside, on the right, there is a small slit window, blocked in the fifteenth century with stones whiter than the surrounding masonry. The insubstantial outer half of this tower has been rebuilt in modern times.

The vanished upper part of the tower, as well as this section of the curtain wall, was reached by a flight of external steps to the left of the door into the tower. To the right,

Little remains of the south gatehouse, whose form is best appreciated from the eighteenth-century illustrations by the Buck brothers (p. 18) and Paul Sandby (inside front cover). The north tower is on the opposite side of the courtyard.

The inner ward is entered through what remains of the fourteenth-century middle gatehouse, built alongside the keep when the castle was rebuilt in stone.

The Middle Gatehouse

The fourteenth-century middle gatehouse almost certainly replaced a Norman gateway in this same position. Both gates would have been approached across, and defended by, the now infilled ringwork ditch. As rebuilt in the fourteenth century, however, the gatehouse projected forward from the Norman curtain, out over the upper scarp of the ditch. Bridge abutments may have been masked when the ditch was filled in. But on the outside of the gate, to the right, a rebated stone at ground level may mark the housing of a hinged drawbridge. On the left, cut into the corner quoin, a small socket might denote the provision of a handrail flanking the bridge.

Now reduced almost to foundation level, the gatehouse was of somewhat makeshift construction. To the left (north), in order to create a straight gate-passage, one side consisted of no more than a wedge of masonry abutting the wall of the Norman keep. To the right, a rectangular tower was placed to the south side of the passage. A projecting stub of the Norman curtain wall, bonded with the original keep, and encased within the wedge of fourteenth-century masonry, is characterized by a predominance of the red conglomerate stone in its core and facing. It contrasts with the uniformly green-grey limestone of the later fabric of the gatehouse.

the curtain runs to meet the masonry of the Norman keep (p. 27). Originally it would have crossed the early ringwork ditch between the inner and outer wards, though all internal traces of this ditch were lost when it was filled in, probably in the early sixteenth century.

THE INNER WARD

The inner ward, always the heart of the medieval castle at Coity, was for the most part enclosed by the faceted Norman curtain wall. To the north, however, a replacement section of wall was built in a straight alignment following the Glyn Dŵr sieges of 1404–05. Internally, the ward is dominated by its two main domestic ranges: the west block, consisting of the fourteenth-century middle gatehouse and the Norman keep with its later annexe; and the south range, incorporating a fourteenth-century hall, kitchen, and latrine tower, together with a fifteenth-century chapel. Between the two ranges is the north-east gatehouse. This tour begins at the middle gate, moving around the ward in a clockwise direction, before leaving through the north-east gatehouse to examine the external features of the castle (pp. 36–7).

A line of stones across the passage may mark the inner face of the drawbridge pit. Some 10 feet (3m) into the gate-passage, a portcullis was positioned in front of the doors. The position of the doors themselves is indicated by their surviving jambs, beyond which a doorway on the right, framed in Sutton stone ashlar, led into the guardchamber or porter's lodge. From a door in the east wall of the guardchamber, entered from the courtyard, a mural staircase (one set within the thickness of the wall) led to the upper levels of the gatehouse.

Between the guardchamber and its outer western wall there is a large rectangular pit. This does not appear to have been a cess-pit, for there is a latrine chute in the south wall of the gate, discharging externally on that wall. It conceivably represents a water cistern, hence the positioning of the gate-tower partly into the ditch. The only other surviving feature in the gate is the narrow loop in its outermost wall.

The Keep

The late twelfth-century Norman keep was built of coursed rubble limestone and many slabs of Triassic conglomerate, with Sutton stone quoins, and a reddish rubble core. It was altered considerably in the fourteenth century, when the middle gatehouse was built to the south and the annexe to the north. Nevertheless, the keep does retain some of its original features. As raised, it consisted

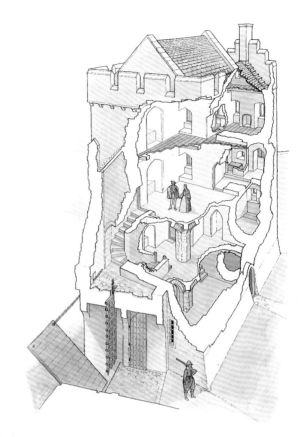

The keep at Coity as it may have appeared following the sixteenth-century refurbishment (Illustration by Chris Jones-Jenkins, after Crown copyright: RCAHMW).

of a basement with two upper floors. A third floor was added in the sixteenth century, at which time the northern annexe was also heightened by another storey. In the late twelfth century, the entrance would have been situated at first-floor level, and there is a suggestion in the Victorian records of G. T. Clark that it lay at the northern end of the east wall. A stub of walling against the south-east corner of the keep may have been part of the external access, but its date is uncertain.

The basement, which to begin with must have been reached from a trap door down from the first floor, is now entered by two breaches in the wall on the courtyard side. The smaller of these was a fourteenth-century doorway. Inside, the basement is dominated by a central octagonal pillar of sandstone ashlar. It was inserted in the 1300s to support rib-vaulted ceilings in both the basement and the first-floor chamber. Prior to this, the floors had been supported on timber beams, as at Ogmore (p. 42).

In the south-east and north-west corners of the basement, there are two Norman slit windows or loops, blocked in the sixteenth century. It was at this time, too, that a staircase was inserted in the north-west

The keep and its adjacent annexe. The remains of the octagonal stone pillar, inserted in the fourteenth century to support the rib-vaulted ceilings of the basement and first-floor chamber, can be seen at first-floor level (Crown copyright: RCAHMW).

corner, and carried up through a breach in the earlier vaulting, with a door or postern (now blocked) set in the north wall at mezzanine level. The function of this door is unclear, but perhaps it provided the Gamages with access to walks and gardens on the north side of the castle.

At first-floor level, the only Norman feature is a narrow Sutton stone light in the north wall, matching that below it in the basement. Holes in the stonework denote a metal grille and wooden shutter. At the base of the octagonal column at this level, part of the fourteenth-century paving over the basement vault still survives, and in the south-west corner are the traces of a Tudor stair to the floor above.

On the second floor, there are scant vestiges of a timber ceiling, and traces of fragmentary window openings represent the general refenestration of the inner ward in the early sixteenth century. Meanwhile, during this Tudor refurbishment, a third floor was added to the keep, again featuring a timber ceiling. The evidence to show that this upper floor was indeed an addition is seen most clearly from the outside, where the reddish Norman masonry, with Sutton stone quoins, meets the grey limestone rubble of the later phase.

High up on the west side of the keep, above the third floor, there is a small section of surviving parapet. Best seen from the outer ward, it is marked by the walling which is carried over four moulded corbels. Until the last century, there was

The courtyard is dominated by the foundations of a very large rectangular structure, the date and function of which are not certain. Beyond is the north-east gatehouse.

evidence for a Tudor chimney in the east wall, no doubt serving fireplaces on the upper floors.

As part of the fourteenth-century refurbishment of the accommodation in the keep, an annexe was added on the north side. This provided a spacious latrine at second-floor level, with a more cramped latrine chamber below. There is, incidentally, no evidence for the Norman-period latrine provision. In the annexe, a vaulted cess-pit at ground level was drained by openings in the west and north walls. The second floor was refenestrated in the sixteenth century, and at the same time the third floor was added, with a small attic above. This third floor had a fireplace between two windows in the north wall, and a latrine was located in a closet in the west wall.

The Courtyard

Within the inner ward courtyard, part of which is flagged with stone slabs, there is a well set just behind the middle gate. But you will notice that the ward as a whole is dominated by the foundations of a very large rectangular structure, which is difficult to date. It clearly predates the later fifteenth-century stair added to the chapel range (p. 31), which overlaps one of its corners. The function and date of the stub of walling running northwards from the building are also uncertain.

On this same side of the ward, the straight section of curtain wall was rebuilt following the siege damage of the early fifteenth century (pp. 14–16). It supports an outer parapet (best seen from

The impressive north-east gatehouse was added in the fifteenth century. Traces of elaborate corbels to support machicolations — murder holes — survive at battlement level.

outside) carried outwards externally on a row of corbels — which were originally the stone treads of a newel staircase. At this point, too, there is a deep pit or cistern enclosed within a section of the curtain.

North-East Gatehouse

Although modest, the fifteenth-century gatehouse in the north-east corner of the inner ward is one of Coity's most impressive surviving features. Standing almost intact, with two upper floors over the gate-passage, it projects boldly from the Norman curtain wall.

The passage was originally vaulted. As you enter it, on the left, there is a door leading to the newel staircase to the upper levels. On the opposite side, although it is now blocked, there was a small lodge for the porter with two windows that overlooked the inner ward. The gate, with large sockets remaining for its drawbar, was near the middle of the passage, and — near the front — you will see the grooves in the side walls for the portcullis.

When it was raised, the portcullis was housed in the well-lit first-floor chamber. This was another stone-vaulted room, and from it a door led out on to the east curtain wall. There was no fireplace at this level, but there was a latrine. The top-floor room provided altogether better accommodation, with ample windows, a fireplace, and a latrine. Before reaching this upper room, the newel stair also gave access to the north curtain wall-walk. It then continued up to the roof level, which featured a 'machicolated' parapet. A latrine on the south-east side of the rooftop would have served those on watch duty.

Before returning to the inner ward, you should leave the castle to examine the exterior of this gatehouse. There are ashlar quoins at the corners, but otherwise it is built of courses of limestone and random rubble. A number of putlog holes for the original scaffolding are visible. The external arch is set within a

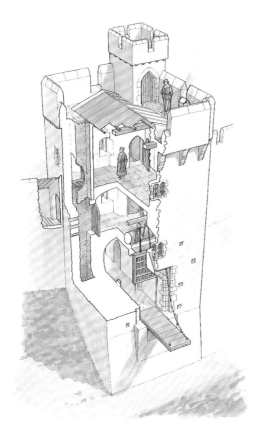

A reconstruction of the north-east gatehouse at Coity as it may have looked in the fifteenth century (Illustration by Chris Jones-Jenkins, after Crown copyright: RCAHMW).

square-headed recess to accommodate the raised drawbridge. The chains or ropes of this drawbridge would have run up from its outermost corners, through the holes in the upper corners of the recess, engaging with a windlass operated on the first floor (see reconstruction, opposite). Above the gate-arch is a spy-hole, now blocked, which opened from the sill of the first-floor window. At battlement level are vestiges of the corbels which would have supported the machicolations or murder holes. Many late medieval towers and gates had these machicolations, notably Raglan Castle in Monmouthshire, built from the 1430s.

The south range of the castle: to the right are the service rooms, in the centre is the principal domestic accommodation dominated by a tall chimney, and to the left is the entrance to the chapel.

THE SOUTH RANGE

Returning to the inner ward, to the left you will see a truncated wall with a central doorway enclosing a small yard or working space. The wall was built in the sixteenth century and originally stood some 18 feet (5.5m) high, as indicated by the stub of masonry against the north-east gatehouse. Beyond the yard lie the remains of the castle chapel.

The Chapel

The basement below the chapel is entered through a doorway leading from the central courtyard, just where there is a patch of surviving paving. Inside the basement, to the immediate left, there is a doorway to a secondary staircase, added soon after the chapel was finally completed in the fifteenth century. To the right, the doorway with the pointed head led from what was originally an external space into the lobby of the main fourteenth-century block.

Sometime after its construction, the chapel basement was divided into three rooms, with the addition of two cross-walls with central doors and small openings. It has been suggested that these rooms served as a pantry or buttery. Three vaulted ribs across the basement carried the timber floor of the chapel above.

At the far end of the basement, to the right, built into the south wall of the grand staircase, there is striking evidence — in the form of a corbel and springer

The east end of the chapel, which was finally completed in the fifteenth century.

— for the intended vaulting of the undercroft of the chapel proposed in the fourteenth century. Had it been completed, the chapel block as a whole would have projected out from the line of the

31

The corbel and springer, built into the south end of the grand stair, indicates that the chapel was originally planned to project beyond the curtain wall.

Had the chapel at Coity been completed to plan, the arrangement may have been similar to that seen here at Kidwelly.

Part of the vaulted passage that ran from the lobby, alongside the main domestic rooms. During the sixteenth century the passage was extended towards the service range.

Norman curtain wall. The arrangements would have been similar to those seen at the late thirteenth-century chapels at Kidwelly, Carmarthenshire, and Restormel in Cornwall, both similar ringwork castles with restricted inner wards for building developments.

Here at Coity, the chapel itself was situated on the first floor. When first completed in the fifteenth century, it could only have been reached from a landing off the grand staircase to the right. Later, access could also be gained by way of the

added stair block in the north-east corner. You will see that the chapel roof-line and the pointed east window were originally lower. The line of the initial roof is marked by its flashing course to each side of the modified window, two-thirds of the way up. With this raising of the window and roof in the fifteenth century, a still discernible section of the parapet and wall-walk was carried round the new gable. Towards the foot of the window, there are slight traces of a stone altar table.

Vaulted Lobby and Passage

With your back to the chapel window, return through the basement and turn left into the pointed fourteenth-century doorway before you reach the entrance from the courtyard. You will enter a vaulted lobby incorporating four doors: one from the chapel basement through which you have entered; one to the right leading into the courtyard; and two to the left, side by side. The first of the left-hand doorways led to the grand staircase, not accessible today as only a few of the original steps survive. Beyond, the second doorway opens into a vaulted passage with a descending flight of steps. These would have provided access to the basement of the projecting chapel as it was planned in the fourteenth century (though never built, pp. 31–2). Modern masonry now partly blocks the lower end of this passage.

A passage which was initially vaulted runs from the lobby along the north side of the main block of rooms. In the sixteenth century, the passage was extended towards the service range, incorporating a new service stair, and with two doorways opening towards the courtyard. One original and one inserted doorway also communicated with the kitchens.

The Service Range

Just beyond, and to the left of the passage, lies the service range. This irregular-shaped range was originally entered from the courtyard through doors at either end. It may have comprised two rooms in the fourteenth century, perhaps separated by a timber partition. But in the sixteenth century — when the domestic buildings in the south range as a whole were being refurbished — the block was divided in two with a masonry cross-wall. This wall allowed for improved kitchen facilities. Externally, towards the courtyard, it incorporates a small arched recess of uncertain

purpose at ground level.

To one side of the cross-wall, the westernmost room of the service range (that closest to the well) contains a double-fireplace and ovens, and there is a blocked Tudor window in the curtain wall.

The easternmost room, entered by both the original door and the one added opposite the new staircase, contains a large malting kiln of uncertain date. To the right of this, notice the drain running out through the curtain wall, and further round there is a fireplace in the inserted sixteenth-century cross-wall.

Above the service area, sockets for floor beams and blocked Tudor windows in the curtain wall indicate two upper floors of domestic accommodation. You will also see a large blocked door at first-floor level in the north wall. Apart from these vestiges, there is little evidence remaining of these apartments, which were clearly extensively refurbished in the sixteenth century. The details are more

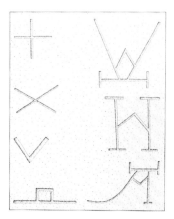

Masons' marks from dressed stone in the south range. Such marks may have been used to identify the work of individual masons (Crown copyright: RCAHMW).

The small arched recess, of uncertain purpose, on the external wall of the service range.

The large malting kiln in the easternmost service room.

A fragment of a grave-slab (now in store), which had been reused in walling in the south range (Crown copyright: RCAHMW).

readily appreciated on the outer face of the curtain (p. 37).

Interestingly, the fourteenth-century builders seem to have incorporated a number of reused fragments of grave-slabs within the walling of the service range. One of these (now in store) bears an incised depiction of a man in civilian clothes.

The Undercroft of the Hall

From the service room which houses the large malting kiln, a doorway leads into the once rib-vaulted undercroft situated beneath the hall. The vault was carried on two central octagonal pillars, the bases of which survive in the floor, as do many of the corbels and springers which supported the vault along the side walls. Three fourteenth-century windows light the undercroft.

In the south-east corner, the substantial doorway leads to a flight of steps which now climb to the upper levels and the latrine tower. However, the staircase is possibly a much later insertion, and originally the doorway may have led along a passage to a postern gate (p. 36). Certainly the steps are later, for in one of the lower treads the builders made use of what is interpreted as a discarded altar-table, incised with crosses.

A view of the undercroft from what would have been the entrance to the hall located above it at first-floor level. The service range can be seen beyond the cross wall.

One of the corbels from which curved ribs sprang to form the vaulted roof of the undercroft of the hall.

It is difficult to appreciate the arrangement of the domestic rooms today, but the windows and fireplaces indicate that a narrow chamber, alongside the first-floor hall, overlooked the courtyard. A second similar chamber was situated on the floor above.

The Hall

Above the undercroft, the hall itself was at the centre of domestic life in the castle. The lords of Coity would have approached what must have been a fine chamber by way of the grand staircase which we have already observed (p. 33).

Standing in the undercroft, you will see what remains of this hall, as well as the rooms on the floors above. Dominating the range are the Tudor chimneys, but the hall windows in the curtain wall survive, although they were altered in the sixteenth century. Part of the hall's east wall also survives, together with a central doorway which gave access into the chamber. A recess south of this doorway may have been a cupboard; a small shaft runs upwards in its rear arch, possibly denoting a bell-rope to summon guests or servants to the hall. The top of this shaft is visible from the landing to the second floor of the latrine tower.

To the north side of the hall, overlooking the inner ward, there was a narrow chamber, with another on the floor above, both equipped with fireplaces.

The Latrine Tower

Now proceed through the doorway in the south-east corner of the undercroft, and climb the stair. The remains of the grand staircase can be seen through a barred gap in the wall. On reaching the first floor, you enter the tower that projects from the south-east section of the curtain wall. Although the ditch and adjacent lengths of curtain wall could be covered by defenders on its battlements, the main purpose of the tower was not defensive. Primarily it housed the latrines serving the domestic range. The lower section of the tower, which served as a large cess-pit, is rectangular within a rounded front. The three upper chambers are oval, their extra width carried out on corbel tables on the west and east sides.

The three upper levels were well lit by windows in the east, west and south walls, and the first- and second-floor rooms contain latrines. There is one opposite the door into the first-floor chamber, whilst the room above has two, one set in an alcove. The first- and second-floor chambers retain their vaults. The chamber on the third floor — now much ruined and not accessible — provided accommodation of some kind, with three

One of the latrines in the tower, which was built to serve the adjacent domestic rooms.

windows and a fireplace on the south-east side of the room. Just before you enter the second floor of the latrine tower, you will see evidence for a door to the right, providing access to the domestic range at this level.

To continue this tour, return to the courtyard and cross the inner ward back to the north-east gatehouse, passing through it and across the modern timber bridge.

EXTERNAL FEATURES OF THE INNER AND OUTER WARDS

Across the ditch are the remains of the outer or counterscarp bank. Standing at the far end of the bridge and facing the castle, immediately to the right and adjoining the gatehouse, there is a short length of the original Norman curtain wall. This meets the rebuilt early fifteenth-century section of curtain which contains a pit or cistern. Beyond, the parapet of this later curtain is supported on a row of corbels formed from the reused newels of a staircase, mentioned above (pp. 29–30). At the end of this curtain wall is the latrine annexe on the north side of the keep, and further to the west is the north tower of the outer ward, the modern grey walling of its rebuilt front clearly discernible from the reddish medieval fabric. The blocked slit in its east wall is also visible.

In the other direction, you will pass the faceted Norman curtain wall, with its distinctive ashlar quoins at the slight changes in angle. The fifteenth-century chapel window is apparent, with the wall-walk rising over the gable above. Then, to the right of the latrine tower, notice an arch at the top of the curtain wall enclosing a murder hole or machicolation slot through which missiles or rocks could be dropped. Below the arch, near the foot of the wall, what resembles a window opening may relate to the postern mentioned earlier (p. 34).

Part of the curtain wall between the north-east gatehouse and the latrine tower. From right to left notice the ashlar quoins marking the change in angles of the curtain, the chapel window and an arch at wall-walk level enclosing a murder hole. Finally, notice how the latrine tower is corbelled out above the rectangular basement in order to create oval chambers.

Indeed, a postern placed here would have been protected by the murder hole above.

On the other side of the latrine tower are the medieval and Tudor windows of the southern domestic range. There are also traces of the original battlements, with a line of drain-holes running between the first and second floors, and vestiges of cross-slits represented by their lower vertical element with an oillet — a circular hole — beneath.

Where the wall of the inner ward meets the outer curtain, there is the base of a fifteenth-century rectangular latrine turret which served the presumed servants' quarters in the domestic block. The wall that runs to the south gatehouse was built at the same time as this turret. It contains eight unusual cross-loops, the vertical slit of each one divided from the horizontal slit by small stones. It seems likely that these loops were designed for use by handgunners. At a later stage, this section of wall was heightened, and the original battlements, encased at that time, are clearly visible. Notice, too, the straight joint in the masonry between the wall and the latrine turret.

Before crossing the bridge to the south tower, note the sluice below the bridge itself, built to control the amount of water in the ditch. Also, at the far end of the outer curtain wall, you can see the buttresses added to support the masonry when the barn was raised in the fifteenth century (p. 16). Finally, in what is now a private garden, there are the remains of the south-west tower.

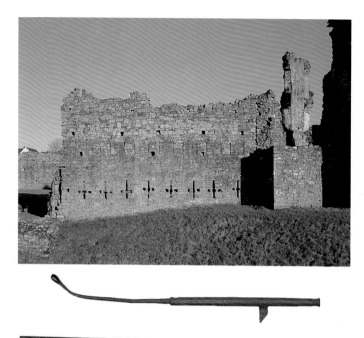

The eight unusual cross-loops in the outer curtain (top) *on the south side of the castle may have been designed for use by handgunners using weapons like those shown here (Copyright: The Board of Trustees of the Armouries, object nos XII.3748, XII.959).*

The south side of the outer curtain. In the distance are the buttresses added to support the curtain when the barn was built in the fifteenth century.

The pretty riverside setting of Ogmore Castle belies its medieval strategic location close to the sea, on the marshy floodplain of the Ewenny and Ogmore rivers.

A TOUR OF OGMORE CASTLE

THE OUTER WARD

The car park alongside the stepping stones which cross the river Ewenny is situated on the south-west side of the castle ringwork defences. From here, return along the approach road, and once you have passed through the gate, you will be entering the stronghold through a break in the rampart of the outer ward.

The Defences

This break in the rampart no doubt marks the site of the original medieval outer gateway. To the left and right, the rampart remains a prominent feature, for here the original earth-and-timber defences doubtless persisted throughout much of the Middle Ages. In contrast, around the inner ward, the rampart was levelled when the curtain wall was built in the early thirteenth century (p. 10).

Although much of the ditch that once fronted the palisaded rampart of the outer bailey has disappeared, a surviving section on the southern side gives a good impression of the original arrangements. To the north, the river probably extended right up to the edge of the castle itself, especially at high tide.

The Masonry Buildings

The only masonry structures which survive in the outer ward lie to the left of the entrance. They represent three phases of the castle's history. The earliest building is denoted by the surviving north-west end of a square or rectangular construction, set against the scarp, and which dates to the early thirteenth century. Of unknown purpose, it was dismantled and overlain by two later structures. The first of these was a late thirteenth-century limekiln, with opposed flues, and a projecting stub of wall abutting one side, possibly used in the charging of the bowl of the kiln. At about the same time as the kiln was built, a small postern with a narrow passage was inserted in the defences on the north-west side of the bailey.

The kiln was eventually abandoned, its vestiges overlain by the building known as the Court House, initially raised sometime in the later Middle Ages and repaired in the early fifteenth century. The main entrance is situated in the long wall on the courtyard side, though its dressed masonry, together with that of the two flanking windows, has long since gone. It was no doubt of the same greenish sandstone used for the framing of the windows in the gable ends, and in the door and window in the north wall. There is also some local Sutton stone in the north doorway. The purpose of this narrow doorway, which is provided with drawbar sockets, was presumably to

The narrow north doorway in the Court House, which presumably allowed access to the postern and river beyond. The stepping stones crossing the Ewenny river are visible through the window.

The inner ward of Ogmore was enclosed with a stone curtain, with a simple gate-tower and wing walls extending into the ditch, early in the thirteenth century. It is the remains of the modified Norman keep, however, which still dominate the site today.

allow access to the Court House from the adjacent postern towards the river.

There is a small single-light window in the western gable, similar to the one by the north door, whereas the window in the eastern gable was of two lights. Both of these windows were fitted with grilles. The windows in the south wall were also of two lights, and all of the openings had deep internal splays so as to provide as much light as possible to the main body of the room.

The height of the roof of the Court House is indicated by the gable ends, which survive almost intact. Beam holes and a single surviving corbel near the top of the long walls are the only evidence for either a ceiling or supports for three roof trusses. However,

the function of the line of small sockets halfway up the west gable is uncertain. One possibility is that they housed joists supporting a small timber gallery.

THE INNER WARD

External Features

Directly opposite the entrance to the outer ward lies the gateway to the inner enclosure, now reached by way of a modern timber bridge. The inner ward as a whole is enclosed by an early thirteenth-century curtain wall, which runs in a series of short straight lengths or facets, like the earlier curtains at both

Coity and Newcastle. At Ogmore, however, there are none of the distinctive ashlar quoins at the angles between the facets seen at the other two sites.

Before passing through the gateway, to left and right you will see wing walls running down from the inner defences across the moat. In the thirteenth century, they would have met the existing timber defences of the outer ward. At the base of these wing walls there are openings for sluices to admit and impound tidal water in the moat around the inner ward. With at least three latrines discharging into it, the moat might also be periodically drained at low tide.

To the left of the inner gateway, projecting from the north-west corner of the main tower or keep, is a secondary rectangular latrine turret. Its latrine chutes discharged through an arched opening at the base, visible externally from the vicinity of the castle car park. At first-floor level, the turret contains a cross-slit, which may have provided some covering fire for the gatehouse, as well as lighting the latrine chamber.

Extending from the latrine turret to the gate is the outer wall of the Norman keep. This was the only part of the early defences to have been built of masonry. Until the thirteenth century, the remaining sections of the inner ward perimeter were surrounded by a bank topped with a timber palisade. Seen from here, the main features of the keep are the two round-headed Norman windows at first-floor level. Above these, there is a prominent course of projecting stones supporting the second floor which was added, along with the latrine turret, in the early thirteenth century.

The Inner Gate-Tower

Approaching the gate, to the left, notice that the secondary masonry clearly abuts the earlier keep. Beneath the modern bridge, the masonry abutment on the outer side of the ditch is modern. On the inner side, however, the thirteenth-century drawbridge pit survives as do the steps that led down into it, though these are now hidden beneath the timber decking. The walling of the original pit may have been extended upwards to carry the

mechanism to operate the bridge. Walls may also have linked the bridge directly to the gate to provide additional security, given that the drawbridge was set at some distance in front of the gate-tower. The gate itself was of a rather simple design with no portcullis. There was a vaulted passage, originally with a double-leaf door opening into the recesses which are clearly visible in the vault above. An

alcove on the left was no doubt the seat used by the porter or sentry, whilst above the vault the stone-slabbed floor of the small first-floor chamber still survives. This was reached from the first floor of the keep, by way of a door inserted in its south-west corner and out along the short stretch of curtain wall linking the two structures. Above the chamber would have been an open battlemented area.

Below the modern timber bridge lies the original drawbridge pit and steps leading down into it.

Double-leaf doors opened into recesses in the vault above the gate passage.

The gate-tower was of a relatively simple arrangement. Beyond the drawbridge the doors opened into a passage with no portcullis or any visible means of defence.

The Keep

Passing through the inner gate, and turning round to your left, you will have a clear view of the interior of the keep, with only its outer wall rising above the basement level. The original entrance, as with most Norman keeps, was at first-floor level. This was doubtless reached by way of an external stair, the position of which is probably indicated by the block of masonry projecting into the courtyard. Alongside this, there is a doorway which was almost certainly a later insertion to provide more convenient access to the basement. Inside, the small enclosed chamber — in what is the southern corner of the basement — was also a later addition, as were the stone benches within the larger area to the right. Notice that these benches are slotted for vertical timbers, possibly for shelving.

Above the basement, in the inner face of the outer wall, the row of joist holes for the beams supporting the first floor are clearly visible. In the twelfth century, this was the main floor of the Norman keep, probably comprising two well-appointed chambers. The walls in both were covered with plaster, which may have been painted. The room to the south was slightly larger, and was lit by the two surviving round-headed windows which have Sutton stone frames. These windows were originally the same size, though the

One of the cushion capitals on the columns that supported the round-headed hood above the fireplace.

sill of that to the right was lowered at some stage.

The two chambers were divided by a partition (probably of timber), the position of which is marked by the projecting stub of ashlar masonry to the right of the larger window. The slightly

When first built, the keep would have been entered at first-floor level via an external stair, probably marked by the block of projecting masonry in the foreground. The row of joist holes marks the floor of the principal chambers and the crease above indicates the line of the original roof, before a second floor was added in the thirteenth century.

smaller northern room was dominated by a handsome fireplace, which had a round-headed hood set on two columns featuring the surviving cushion capitals. As completed in the twelfth century, there was a window in the north wall of this room, situated just to the right of the later door into the latrine turret. But as part of the thirteenth-century improvements, the window was enlarged to serve as a doorway giving access to the curtain wall. A timber walk-way must have been erected across the external angle, and the arrangement would have mirrored the link between the keep and the inner gateway already noted above (p. 41).

The line of the original Norman roof over the keep is marked by the long slot which runs along the length of the surviving outer wall. This slot terminates at each end with a socket for a timber beam. Above this slot are the remains of the thirteenth-century second floor, the main surviving feature of which is a modest fireplace whose flue made use of the Norman chimney. When this addition was made, the facilities were improved with the addition of the latrine turret which clasps the north-west corner of the keep (p. 41). As part of the new arrangements, a newel staircase was inserted into the existing fabric in this same corner of the building. This provided communication between the first and second floors, and also gave access to the latrines at each level in the projecting turret. The stair would have continued upwards to roof level.

The site of the hall added to the northern side of the inner ward in the thirteenth century. The kitchen may have been located at its western end, close to the keep.

The Hall and Possible Kitchen Area

Leaving the keep, the foundations of the large rectangular building overlooking the river are the remains of the thirteenth-century hall block. You will see that the builders utilized the stone curtain for its north and east walls. To accommodate the building within the curtain and wall-walk, the hall may have been located at ground-floor level rather than the more familiar first-floor arrangement with a basement below. Following its completion, it would have taken over from the keep as the centre of domestic life in the castle. Although there is no fireplace in any of its walls, a central hearth was discovered during clearance work at the site.

Most of the south wall represents a late medieval rebuild of the hall. On this side there are traces of three small windows and two doorways. The easternmost door was clearly the main entrance, being secured by a drawbar, the socket for which is now blocked. The shutters for the window in the east gable wall were also secured against an iron grille by a drawbar. The door in the north wall of the basement is a later insertion.

The grassed area in the angle between the hall and the keep may be the site of the main castle kitchen. It would certainly have been in a convenient position here, and the foundations of a structure were located during the initial conservation work on the ruins. A small recess in the curtain wall may have been related to such a kitchen, and the offset which runs along the wall, together with a stone corbel, may mark the line of the roof of the lost building.

A PRE-NORMAN INSCRIBED STONE

During the initial clearance and conservation of Ogmore Castle, workers found a pre-Norman inscribed stone built into a nineteenth-century limekiln in the 'cellar' building (p. 45). The original is now at the National Museum & Gallery, Cardiff, though you will find a replica in the corner of the inner ward, located between the keep and the hall. The stone is thought to date from the early eleventh century, and presumably comes from the immediate vicinity. Part of the Latin inscription survives, to read on one side: 'Be it [known to all men] that Arthmail gave (this) field to God and Glywys and Nertat and his daughter'. On another side may be read: '[In the name] of God Most High, the cross of …'.

The pre-Norman inscribed stone, which was found during clearance work at Ogmore and is now in the National Museum & Gallery, Cardiff (National Museum of Wales).

The Eastern Range and Cellar

In the east curtain wall, close to the south-east corner of the hall, there was a small doorway or postern, fitted with a drawbar, introduced in the thirteenth century. This door may have allowed access to a small harbour below, at the point where the moat widens sufficiently for small vessels to have docked and unloaded supplies at high tide. In the later Middle Ages, this minor entrance was blocked in order to accommodate a fireplace which stood in a building running south from the hall to the 'cellar'. The roof-line of this structure is clearly marked by the line of projecting stones in the curtain wall. To the west, beneath the turf, there are the foundations of another medieval structure found during consolidation of the castle (see ground plan).

To the south of both of these, the so-called 'cellar' building is a somewhat enigmatic structure, the purpose of which remains uncertain. With its entry facing the keep, the masonry consists largely of coursed rubble, though with fine squared quoins. A barrel-vaulted passage leads down to the basement, where the ashlar framing of the doorway provides further evidence for a twelfth-century date of construction. Moreover, the dating is confirmed by the unusual arrangement of the steps. Originally the basement was entered from the lower level of the initial courtyard, down the three bottom steps. But when, in the early thirteenth century, the interior of the inner ward was raised with spoil thrown down from the rampart prior to the construction of the curtain wall, an upper flight of five steps was added to the arrangement. These abut the Norman steps in a rather awkward fashion.

Although the masonry of the vaulted passage leading down to the basement abuts the 'cellar', both appear to be contemporary Norman work. At first, the basement itself had windows set high in the northern and southern walls, with a narrow doorway in the east wall. The northern window was later converted into another door.

The 'cellar' has been interpreted as the massive substructure of a timber tower. However, it seems likely that

The northern window of the cellar was later converted into a doorway.

The 'cellar' remains an enigmatic structure. Built in the late twelfth century, its function is uncertain, though it seems likely that the basement at least was used for storage.

the upper storey was also of masonry, and although there is evidence for a timber sleeper beam exposed in the truncated walling in the north-west wall, this may have simply provided extra reinforcement, comparable to that observed in medieval masonry buildings elsewhere in Britain. Evidence for the 'cellar' being built later than the keep is based on the assumption that two pieces of loose carved stone were in fact derived from the fabric of the 'cellar'. Comparable with designs seen in the late twelfth-century gateway at Newcastle (pp. 49–50), these stone fragments may be seen reset in the south face of the late medieval wall which runs between the east wall of the 'cellar' and the east curtain wall. As for the function of the surviving basement of the 'cellar', its high windows and the absence of a fireplace suggest that it was probably used for storage.

In the later Middle Ages two small chambers were added to the west front of the 'cellar', flanking the passage to the basement. In the nineteenth century, a limekiln was constructed within the building, presumably producing lime for agricultural purposes. Indeed, this might well explain the truncated state of so much of the castle's fabric today.

One of the two fragments of carved stone reset into the late medieval wall between the 'cellar' and east curtain. Similar in style to the gateway at Newcastle, these fragments are assumed to have come from the 'cellar' and have been used to date its construction.

The Southern Range

On the south side of the inner ward are the footings of a rectangular building which was divided into three units. Designated as 'offices', the true purpose of the block is unknown. Only one of the internal cross-walls

One of two latrines in the eastern curtain, which was accessed directly from the courtyard.

survives, though the remains of door jambs show that both were pierced by a doorway at their southern end. The form of one jamb is comparable to that of the later-medieval work in the hall. The purpose of the external feature with a recess or slot, at the south-west corner, is also uncertain.

The Curtain Wall

The southern side of the inner ward, near the 'office' range, is a good position from which to appreciate the early thirteenth-century curtain wall. The best preserved sections, with some of the wall-walk and parapet still evident, run from the south-west corner around to the hall, although there is a break in the middle. The

eastern facet of the curtain incorporates two turrets, both of which house two latrines that discharged into the moat. That to the north appears to have been accessed directly from the courtyard; in contrast, the more southerly example probably served sentries on duty at wall-walk level, though much of the detail was obscured when the curtain wall was later rebuilt. The details of the latrines are best appreciated from the outside, on the castle bank.

Numerous sockets, which you will observe in the curtain wall, are known as putlog holes. These would have housed the scaffolding timbers used during the construction of the castle. They would have been blocked up upon completion of the work, but water and frost action over the years have reopened the voids.

The east curtain and 'office' range.

A BIRD'S-EYE VIEW OF OGMORE CASTLE
FROM THE SOUTH-WEST

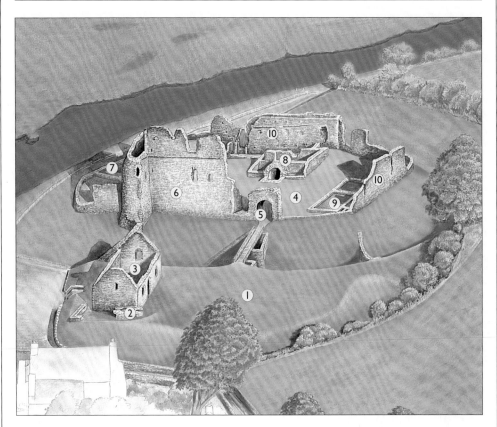

1 Outer ward — *the outer defences were never rebuilt in stone and parts of the earthwork rampart survive. Originally, there would have been a timber palisade and timber buildings in the outer ward, but only the remains of three stone structures now survive (pp. 10–11, 39–40).*

2 Limekiln — *dating from the late thirteenth-century, this structure overlies an earlier rectangular building and was probably used for the production of building mortar (p. 39).*

3 Court House — *identified as the building substantially repaired in 1454–55, the origins of the Court House could go back to the previous century, when it may have been used as a chapel (pp. 14, 39–40).*

4 Inner ward — *surrounded by a tidal moat, the level of the interior of the inner ward was raised when the earthwork defences were flattened to make way for the curtain walls, early in the thirteenth century. (pp. 10, 40–1).*

5 Inner gate-tower — *a simple two-storey gate-tower closed by a pair of heavy doors, but no portcullis. A drawbridge in front provided some additional protection (p. 41).*

6 Keep — *raised as a two-storey building in the twelfth century, the keep was entered at first-floor level from the courtyard. The single large chamber was probably divided into two by a timber partition. Another floor was added in the thirteenth century, together with a latrine turret (pp. 8, 42–3).*

7 Hall — *built against the curtain wall in the thirteenth century, the single-storey hall block was later substantially modified (pp. 10, 43).*

8 'Cellar' — *a substantial late twelfth-century stone-built structure of unknown purpose (pp. 9, 44–5).*

9 Southern range — *designated 'offices', the true purpose of this later medieval block of three rooms is not known (p. 46).*

10 Curtain wall — *built in short straight sections in the thirteenth century, the curtain wall still stands to wall-walk level in places. Two wing walls across the moat helped strengthen the defences and control the flow of water (pp. 10, 40).*

(Illustration by Dale Evans)

The striking Norman gateway to Newcastle. The distinctive decoration has been dated to about 1150–80, during the lordship of Earl William of Gloucester. It could, however, belong to the period when King Henry II held Newcastle, between 1183 and 1188.

A TOUR OF NEWCASTLE

The gate into the grounds at Newcastle brings you to the south-west side of the stronghold, but before entering through the striking Norman gateway, it is worth looking at some of the external details on this side.

Exterior of the South Tower and the Curtain Wall

The approach is dominated by the remains of a square tower which straddles the south curtain wall and still stands to a considerable height. Both the tower and the curtain have had most of the lower courses of their ashlar facing removed in the recent past, including the dressed stonework from a continuous battered plinth. Above this, the wall facing of the curtain survives, generally constructed of coursed rubble, though with finer ashlar around the gateway. Traces of the ashlar of the battered plinth survive in the corners where the tower meets the curtain wall. This fine ashlar was Sutton stone, quarried not far from Ogmore, at Southerndown. The other dressed stone visible on the outer face of the south tower is a greenish sandstone — vestiges of the sixteenth-century window inserted on the first floor.

East of the Norman gateway, the curtain with its battered plinth runs in a straight line, before turning through a right angle to run north along a steep escarpment. Then, from the north-east corner, it continues in a series of facets back to the south tower. There is another mural tower in the centre of the western side of the castle. Internally, the curtain wall still stands somewhere between about 17 and 20 feet (5.2m and 6.3m). As completed in the twelfth century, the wall would have been considerably higher, rising to its now vanished wall-walk and crenellated battlements. The square sockets you will see scattered about the walls are putlog holes. These would have secured scaffolding during the construction of the castle, and would have been blocked once the building had been completed.

The Gateway

Flanked by the south tower, the gateway with its distinctive decoration is undoubtedly the most outstanding feature of the castle. The steps up to it are modern, and you will find that it is plain on the inside, but it stands as one of the most significant pieces of late-Romanesque work in the area. Raised entirely in ashlar, the outer arch has a rounded head with a roll moulding springing from weathered capitals, each of a different design. The composition frames a recessed segmental inner arch which carries greater embellishment. Here, roll mouldings alternate with sunken rectangular panels containing strips of pellets, a

Newcastle stands on an escarpment well above the river Ogmore, with widespread views across the valley to Coity and the hills of the Blaenau beyond.

A detail of the Newcastle gateway showing roll mouldings alternating with sunken panels containing strips of pellets.

The south doorway of Quenington church, Gloucestershire, to which the decoration at Newcastle has been compared.

rare decoration apparently only paralleled in the south doorway at Quenington church in Gloucestershire.

Passing through the gateway, you will see sockets within the flanking walls. These would have housed the timber drawbar used to secure a wooden two-leaf door.

The South Tower

Once through the gateway, turn to your left to look at the internal details of the south tower. The ground-floor doorway and adjoining window in the north wall are probably sixteenth-century features, replacing original examples in these same positions. In fact, there are certainly traces of a ground-floor Norman door similarly placed in the south-east corner of the west tower.

The other ground-floor feature in the south tower is the fireplace situated in the west wall. This was one of the modifications made during the Tudor refurbishment of the castle. Opposing sockets in the sides of the fireplace presumably housed an iron crossbar to support cooking pots suspended over the flames. In the sixteenth century, then, this room may have served as the kitchen for those in residence on the upper floors of the tower. Large square sockets in the north and south walls formerly held the main beams supporting the first floor.

Leaving the tower and turning left, you can see that access to the first floor was gained by way of an external staircase on the west side, in the angle between the tower and curtain wall. This has been renewed. At first-floor level you can see inserted Tudor windows in the south and north walls, and a Norman fireplace in the east wall. Beside the north window, a recess contains the remains of a newel stair which led to the second floor. Scant traces of two more inserted Tudor windows survive to the north and south on this upper floor. A medieval fireplace is also clearly visible in the east wall, to the right of which another window overlooks the gateway.

The Bailey or Courtyard

Moving clockwise around the bailey, on the west side you will find the remains of the second and slightly larger square tower. Only the ground floor or basement survives, with one slit window in its outer west wall. Lacking a fireplace, and presumably serving as a storeroom, it was originally entered from the courtyard through a door at the south-east corner. Like its southern counterpart, this tower straddled the curtain above a battered plinth, though here the plinth was not restricted to the front but also extended around the rear of the tower. The outer half of the tower, and no doubt the infilled ditch, now lie in a private garden.

On the north side of the bailey, there are the freestanding footings of the eastern half of a building, its north-eastern corner buttressed by a fragment of secondary wall. The date of this structure is uncertain, though it is likely to be late medieval — or possibly even part of the Tudor refurbishment.

In earlier centuries, the main domestic buildings at Newcastle were the successive halls ranged in a line against

THE TWELVE KNIGHTS AND THE CONQUEST OF GLAMORGAN

One of the most enduring stories of medieval Glamorgan is the account of how Robert fitz Hamo, in the company of twelve knights, conquered the area in 1091.

The account, entitled 'The winning of the Lordship of Glamorgan out of Welshmen's hands', was first compiled between 1561 and 1566 by Sir Edward Stradling (1529–1609) of St Donat's Castle, Glamorgan. In it, he names fitz Hamo's twelve companions, including a certain William de Esterling, whose descendants were better known

There is no doubt of Robert fitz Hamo's role in the conquest of Glamorgan, but the identity of his companions is less certain. This early sixteenth-century illustration of Robert is taken from a book of benefactors of Tewkesbury Abbey (Bodleian Library, Ms. Top. Glouc., d. 2, f.13r).

by the name of Stradling. The account seems to have reached Blanche Parry — a relative of the Stradlings and a lady-in-waiting to Queen Elizabeth I (1558–1603) — from whom it came into the hands of the Tudor historian, David Powel. In 1584, Powel gave the account much wider currency and permanence by including it in his influential book, *Historie of Cambria*.

Of fitz Hamo's role in the conquest of Glamorgan there is no doubt, but there is less certainty and more fable regarding his twelve companions. Some of the names of the knights did make an early appearance in the records for south Wales. For example, William de Londres (Ogmore) is known by 1114, the Umfravilles (Penmark) were certainly in Glamorgan by 1129, the le Sors (Peterston) are recorded in about 1102, witnessing charters in Gwynllŵg, as are the St Quentins (Llanblethian). Of the remaining knights, however, including William de Esterling, there is no trace until the later twelfth and thirteenth centuries.

Stradling's fictional ancestry was created out of a desire to extend the family lineage back to the Norman conquest of Glamorgan and thereby demonstrate his family's ancient origins and rights within the county. Alas the claim cannot be substantiated for the Stradling family arrived from what is now Switzerland no earlier than the reign of Edward I (1272–1307). Thereafter the rise of the family in Glamorgan was rapid.

Sir Edward Stradling (d. 1609), who is commemorated in this marble monument in St Donat's church, was responsible for naming his own ancestor as one of fitz Hamo's fictitious companions (Rector and Churchwardens, St Donat's Church).

The title page of David Powel's Historie of Cambria, in which Sir Edward Stradling's tale first appeared in print in 1584 (National Museum of Wales).

the east curtain wall. These are now reduced to their footings. The earliest of the two halls is that to the south, with a doorway in its northern wall. This building was probably associated with the original earth-and-timber ringwork at the site, which explains why its original south and east walls were removed when the late twelfth-century curtain was constructed. The width of the hall suggests that it may have been aisled. The rounded corners of its surviving north end were presumably matched in the missing areas, giving it the characteristic form of a number of other early Norman castle halls in this region (p. 5).

The narrower and later hall to the north, with its central hearth (now marked by fragments of a millstone), was probably built in the thirteenth century. The parallel partition walls inserted into the Norman

The remains of two halls can be seen in the courtyard of Newcastle. The south tower is located to the right of the entrance.

hall may date from the same time. You will see two thickenings of masonry on the east side of the later hall against the curtain wall. That closest to the curtain is the east wall of the hall against which there is a second thickening for internal benching. A section of benching also survives against the west wall. A doorway was

sited near the north-west corner of the building.

In the nineteenth century, the castle scholar, G. T. Clark, recorded the vestiges of a keep near the middle of the courtyard. From this point, if you look over the east curtain, you should be able to see Coity Castle in the middle distance.

FURTHER READING

The text of this guidebook is largely derived from the survey of the early castles of Glamorgan by the Royal Commission on the Ancient and Historical Monuments of Wales. The authors and Cadw would like to thank the Commission and also Professor R. R. Davies and Professor R. A. Griffiths for their assistance.

G. T. Clark, *Mediaeval Military Architecture*, 2 volumes (London 1884).

David Crouch, 'The Slow Death of Kingship in Glamorgan, 1067–1158', *Morgannwg*, **79** (1985), 20–41.

R. R. Davies, *Conquest, Coexistence and Change: Wales 1063–1415* (Oxford 1987); reprinted in paperback as, *The Age of Conquest: Wales 1063–1415* (Oxford 1991).

R. R. Davies, *The Revolt of Owain Glyn Dŵr* (Oxford 1995).

Ralph A. Griffiths, 'The Norman Conquest and the Twelve Knights of Glamorgan', in Ralph A. Griffiths, *Conquerors and Conquered in Medieval Wales* (Stroud 1994), 19–29 .

John R. Kenyon, 'Castle Studies and G. T. Clark, with Particular Reference to Wales and the Marches', in Brian Ll. James, editor, *G. T. Clark: Scholar Ironmaster in the Victorian Age* (Cardiff 1998), 83–102.

T. B. Pugh, editor, *Glamorgan County History, Volume III: The Middle Ages* (Cardiff 1971).

The Royal Commission on Ancient and Historical Monuments in Wales, *An Inventory of the Ancient Monuments in Glamorgan, Volume III, Part 1a: The Early Castles* (London 1991).

Peter White, 'Castle Gateways During the Reign of Henry II', *Antiquaries Journal*, **76** (1996), 241–47.

Glanmor Williams, *Recovery, Reorientation and Reformation: Wales c. 1415–1642* (Oxford 1987); reprinted in paperback as, *Renewal and Reformation: Wales c. 1415–1642* (Oxford 1993).